· EX LIBRIS ·

BIRDS & BLOOMS

of the 50 States

BIRDS & BLOOMS

of the 50 States

By Anna Branning and Mara Murphy

CHRONICLE BOOKS

SAN FRANCISCO

Library of Congress Cataloging-in-Publication Data available.

ISBN: 978-1-4521-1263-3

Manufactured in China.

This book contains reproductions of letterpress artwork.
To purchase a letterpress print, please visit www.dutchdoorpress.com

10 9 8 7 6 5 4 3 2 1

Chronicle Books LLC
680 Second Street
San Francisco, CA 94107
www.chroniclebooks.com

INTRODUCTION

When, in 2008, we began the letterpress print series that would ultimately become *Birds & Blooms of the 50 States* we didn't quite grasp the magnitude of what we were undertaking, nor did we fully realize what a significant project it would turn out to be. The idea came to us a year after we started our greeting card company, Dutch Door Press. Our card designs featured a variety of graphic flower shapes and nonspecific birds. But the more we used nature as a source of inspiration, the more we wanted to set ourselves the challenge of featuring real and specific flowers and birds in our work. It occurred to us one day that we could depict the U.S. state symbols—pairing them in prints that featured the birds and flowers selected to represent each state. We quickly got excited about the prospect of creating prints that were both grounded in reality and truly meaningful, both to us personally and to a wide audience of people born, raised, and living in these places. We started with states that had personal significance for us, the states where we were born—Mara in Pennsylvania, Anna in Texas—and California, where our children were born. We spent countless hours with every pairing of bloom and bird, studying everything from the way state symbols are selected to the biological features of each species and then sketching repeatedly until we arrived at a final design for each pair that we ultimately printed by hand on our antique printing press. Four years and fifty states later, we were done! We very much hope that our work here will conjure memories of the special and meaningful places in your own life. And we hope that you enjoy this book as much as we have enjoyed making it.

—Anna Branning & Mara Murphy

ALABAMA

Received statehood in: 1819
The 22nd U.S. state
State population in 1910: 2,138,093
State population in 2010: 4,779,736
State nickname: The Yellowhammer State (unofficial)
State capital: Montgomery

State bird common name: Yellowhammer woodpecker
Scientific name: Colaptes auratus L.
Also known as: Northern flicker
Year adopted as the state bird: 1927
Fun fact: Although it was officially made the state
bird in 1927, the yellowhammer had been considered
the state bird unofficially since the Civil War period,
during which Alabama's Confederate soldiers were
nicknamed Yellowhammers.

State flower common name: Camellia
Scientific name: Camellia japonica L.
Year adopted as the state flower: 1959
Chosen for: Large, beautiful blooms and abundance
Fun fact: Prior to 1959, the state flower was the
goldenrod, which was adopted in 1927.

Other state symbols:
State tree: Southern longleaf pine
State mammal: Black bear

"Alabama"
Yellowhammer & Camellia

ALASKA

Received statehood in: 1959
The 49th U.S. state
State population in 1910: 63,592
State population in 2010: 710,231
State nickname: The Last Frontier
State capital: Juneau

State bird common name: Willow ptarmigan
Scientific name: Lagopus lagopus
Year adopted as the state bird: 1955
Fun fact: The willow ptarmigan's feathers change from
brown in the warmer months to white in the colder
months, a camouflage adaptation.

State flower common name: Alpine forget-me-not
Scientific name: Myosotis alpestris
Year adopted as the state flower: 1959
Fun fact: The forget-me-not had been considered
emblematic of the Alaska Territory and became the
state flower officially once Alaska became a state.

Other state symbols:
State tree: Sitka spruce
State land mammal: Moose
State marine mammal: Bowhead whale

"Alaska"
Willow Ptarmigan & Forget-Me-Not

ARIZONA

Received statehood in: 1912
The 48th U.S. state
State population in 1910: 122,931
State population in 2010: 6,392,017
State nickname: The Grand Canyon State
State capital: Tuscon

State bird common name: Cactus wren
Scientific name: Campylorhynchus brunneicapillus
Year adopted as the state bird: 1931
Fun fact: The cactus wren builds a large, football-shaped nest among the thorns of a cactus, most commonly, the saguaro.

State flower common name: Saguaro cactus blossom
Scientific name: Carnegiea gigantea
Year adopted as the state flower: 1931
Chosen for: Native to the desert of Arizona
Fun fact: The blooms, which give off a pungent scent, have a short life of less than twenty-four hours. They develop into edible fruit.

Other state symbols:
State tree: Palo verde
State mammal: Ringtail

"Arizona"
Cactus Wren & Saguaro Cactus Blossom

ARKANSAS

Received statehood in: 1836
The 25th U.S. state
State population in 1910: 1,574,449
State population in 2010: 2,915,918
State nickname: The Natural State
State capital: Little Rock

State bird common name: Mockingbird
Scientific name: Mimus polyglottos
Year adopted as the state bird: 1929
Fun fact: The mockingbird gets its common and
Latin names from its ability to mimic the songs
of other birds.

State flower common name: Apple blossom
Scientific name: Pyrus malus
Year adopted as the state flower: 1901
Fun fact: Once a major apple-producing state, Arkansas
hosts an annual apple festival in the town of Lincoln.

Other state symbols:
State tree: Pine
State mammal: White-tailed deer

"Arkansas"
Mockingbird & Apple Blossom

CALIFORNIA

Received statehood in: 1850
The 31st U.S. state
State population in 1910: 2,377,549
State population in 2010: 37,253,956
State nickname: The Golden State
State capital: Sacramento

State bird common name: California valley quail
Scientific Name: Lophortyx californicus
Year adopted as the state bird: 1931
Chosen by: The Audubon Society
Fun fact: The California valley quail is most common in
California, Oregon, Washington, and Baja California,
but also ranges widely along the Pacific Coast from
Mexico into southern British Columbia.

State flower common name: California poppy
Scientific name: Eschscholzia californica
Year adopted as the state flower: 1903
Also known as: Flame flower, cup of gold, golden poppy
Fun fact: Once prized by California's Native Americans
as a food source, today the California poppy is
protected by state law. It is illegal to pick or destroy
the plant.

Other state symbols:
State tree: California redwood
State mammal: Grizzly bear

"California"
California Valley Quail & California Poppy

COLORADO

Received statehood in: 1876
The 38th U.S. state
State population in 1910: 799,024
State population in 2010: 5,029,196
State nickname: The Centennial State
State capital: Denver

State bird common name: Lark bunting
Scientific name: Calamospiza melanocorys
Also known as: Prairie lark finch
Year adopted as the state bird: 1931

State flower common name: Rocky Mountain columbine
Scientific name: Aquilegia coerulea
Year adopted as the state flower: 1899
Fun fact: A state law passed in 1925 protects the rare
and delicate flower by limiting the number of stems,
buds, or blossoms a person can pick to twenty-five
per day.

Other state symbols:
State tree: Colorado blue spruce
State mammal: Rocky Mountain bighorn sheep

"Colorado"
Lark Bunting & Rocky Mountain Columbine

CONNECTICUT

Received statehood in: 1788
The 5th U.S. state
State population in 1910: 1,114,756
State population in 2010: 3,574,097
State nickname: The Constitution State
State capital: Hartford

State bird common name: American Robin
Scientific name: Turdus migratorius
Also known as: North American robin
Year adopted as the state bird: 1943
Fun fact: The robin is actually a thrush, but was named
by English colonists after the red-breasted robin native
to the British Isles.

State flower common name: Mountain laurel
Scientific name: Kalmia latifolia
Year adopted as the state flower: 1907
Fun fact: The mountain laurel is a relative of the
blueberry and grows to a height of five to fifteen feet.

Other state symbols:
State tree: Charter Oak
State mammal: Sperm whale

"Connecticut"
American Robin & Mountain Laurel

DELAWARE

Received statehood in: 1787
The 1st U.S. state
State population in 1910: 202,322
State population in 2010: 897,934
State nickname: The First State
State capital: Dover

State bird common name: Blue hen chicken
Scientific name: Gallus gallus
Year adopted as the state bird: 1939
Fun fact: The blue hen chicken was selected as the state bird because of its historical ties to valiant Revolutionary War soldiers who were compared to the hens, also esteemed for their fighting abilities.

State flower common name: Peach blossom
Scientific name: Prunus persica
Year adopted as the state flower: 1895
Fun fact: The peach blossom was chosen as state flower because, at the time, Delaware was a major producer of peaches, boasting more than 800,000 peach trees in her orchards.

Other state symbols:
State tree: American holly
State animal: Horseshoe crab

"Delaware"
Blue Hen Chicken & Peach Blossom

DISTRICT OF COLUMBIA

Founded in: 1790
The capital of the United States of America
Population in 1910: 331,069
Population in 2010: 601,723
Also known as: Washington, D.C.
Nickname: D.C.

Symbolic bird common name: Wood thrush
Scientific name: Hylocichla mustelina
Year adopted: 1938
Fun fact: A wood thrush can split its voice into two
harmonious notes at the same time.

Symbolic flower common name: American beauty rose
Scientific name: Rosa 'American Beauty'
Year adopted: Unknown
Fun fact: Originally from France, this fragrant hybrid
rose can grow up to fifteen feet tall.

Other symbols:
Tree: Scarlet oak
Song: "The Star-Spangled Banner"

"District of Columbia"
Wood Thrush & American Beauty Rose

FLORIDA

Received statehood in: 1845
The 27th U.S. state
State population in 1910: 752,619
State population in 2010: 18,801,310
State nickname: The Sunshine State
State capital: Tallahassee

State bird common name: Mockingbird
Scientific name: Mimus polyglottos
Year adopted as the state bird: 1927
Fun fact: This songbird that resides in Florida year-round will often sing all night long, especially in the springtime.

State flower common name: Orange blossom
Scientific name: Citrus sinensis
Year adopted as the state flower: 1909
Fun fact: The orange blossom was chosen for its fragrance and beauty, and because of the state's large orange production.

Other state symbols:
State tree: Sabal palm
State animal: Florida panther

"Florida"
Mockingbird & Orange Blossom

GEORGIA

Received statehood in: 1788
The 4th U.S. state
State population in 1910: 2,609,121
State population in 2010: 9,687,653
State nickname: The Peach State
State capital: Atlanta

State bird common name: Brown thrasher
Scientific name: Toxostoma rufum
Year adopted as the state bird: 1970
Fun fact: Unofficially declared the state bird in 1935
by the governor, the brown thrasher became an official
symbol of the state in 1970.

State flower common name: Cherokee rose
Scientific name: Rosa laevigata
Year adopted as the state flower: 1916
Fun fact: Native to southern China, the Cherokee
rose was named for the Native American tribe that
was responsible for spreading the plant throughout
Georgia.

Other state symbols:
State tree: Live oak
State mammal: Right whale

"Georgia"
Brown Thrasher & Cherokee Rose

HAWAII

Received statehood in: 1959
The 50th U.S. state
State population in 1910: 191,874
State population in 2010: 1,360,301
State nickname: The Aloha State
State capital: Honolulu

State bird common name: Nene
Scientific name: Branta sandvicensis
Year adopted as the state bird: 1957
Also known as: Hawaiian goose
Fun fact: The Hawaiian goose is a unique species found only on the Hawaiian Islands.

State flower: Yellow hibiscus
Scientific name: Hibiscus brackenridgei
Year adopted as the state flower: 1988
Fun fact: When the hibiscus was originally selected to symbolize Hawaii, no particular flower was specified. In 1988, the yellow hibiscus was designated as the state flower because it is native to the Hawaiian Islands.

Other state symbols:
State tree: Kukul
State mammal: Hawaiian monk seal

"Hawaii"
Nene & Yellow Hibiscus

IDAHO

Received statehood in: 1890
The 43rd U.S. state
State population in 1910: 325,594
State population in 2010: 1,567,582
State nickname: The Gem State
State capital: Boise

State bird common name: Mountain bluebird
Scientific name: Sialia currucoides
Year adopted as the state bird: 1931
Fun fact: A second bird symbol of Idaho is the state
raptor, the peregrine falcon.

State flower common name: Syringa
Scientific name: Philadelphus lewisii
Year adopted as the state flower: 1931
Also known as: Mock orange
Fun fact: The syringa was adopted as the state flower
after it had been incorporated into the state seal
following a competition by local artists.

Other state symbols:
State tree: Western white pine
State horse: Appaloosa

"Idaho"
Mountain Bluebird & Syringa

ILLINOIS

Received statehood in: 1818
The 21st U.S. state
State population in 1910: 5,638,591
State population in 2010: 12,830,632
State nickname: The Prairie State
State capital: Springfield

State bird common name: Cardinal
Scientific name: Richmondena cardinalis cardinalis
Year adopted as the state bird: 1929
Also know as: Northern cardinal
Fun fact: Before being named officially by the state
legislature, the cardinal was chosen by schoolchildren
as the state bird.

State flower common name: Violet
Scientific name: Viola sororia
Year adopted as the state flower: 1908
Fun fact: The purple iris was considered as an option
for the state flower designation, but violet was selected
instead.

Other state symbols:
State tree: White oak
State animal: White-tailed deer

"Illinois"
Cardinal & Violet

INDIANA

Received statehood in: 1816
The 19th U.S. state
State population in 1910: 2,700,876
State population in 2010: 6,483,802
State nickname: The Hoosier State
State capital: Indianapolis

State bird common name: Cardinal
Scientific name: Richmondena cardinalis cardinalis
Year adopted as the state bird: 1933
Fun fact: The cardinal does not migrate, and its brilliant red plumes are highly visible all winter.

State flower common name: Peony
Scientific name: Paeonia
Year adopted as the state flower: 1957
Fun fact: Prior to 1957, the state flower was the zinnia.

Other state symbols:
State tree: Tulip poplar
State stone: Limestone

"Indiana"
Cardinal & Peony

IOWA

Received statehood in: 1846
The 29th U.S. state
State population in 1910: 2,224,771
State population in 2010: 3,046,355
State nickname: The Hawkeye State
State capital: Des Moines

State bird common name: American goldfinch
Scientific name: Carduelis tristis
Year adopted as the state bird: 1933
Also known as: Eastern goldfinch, wild canary
Fun fact: The American goldfinch is the only member of
the finch family that replaces its entire set of feathers at
least once a year.

State flower common name: Rose
Scientific name: Rosa
Year adopted as the state flower: 1897
Fun fact: The wild prairie rose is commonly known as
the state's flower symbol, although no specific species
has been officially designated.

Other state symbols:
State tree: Oak
State rock: Geode

"Iowa"
American Goldfinch & Rose

KANSAS

Received statehood in: 1861
The 34th U.S. state
State population in 1910: 1,690,949
State population in 2010: 2,853,118
State nickname: The Sunflower State
State capital: Topeka

State bird common name: Western meadowlark
Scientific name: Sturnella neglecta
Year adopted as the state bird: 1937
Fun fact: The western meadowlark's diet consists mainly of insects dug from the ground.

State flower common name: Sunflower
Scientific name: Helianthus annuus
Year adopted as the state flower: 1903
Fun fact: The modern sunflower is the result of nearly 3,000 years of cultivation by Native Americans.

Other state symbols:
State tree: Cottonwood
State mammal: American buffalo

"Kansas"
Western Meadowlark & Sunflower

KENTUCKY

Received statehood in: 1792
The 15th U.S. state
State population in 1910: 2,289,905
State population in 2010: 4,339,367
State nickname: The Bluegrass State
State capital: Frankfort

State bird common name: Cardinal
Scientific name: Richmondena cardinalis cardinalis
Year adopted as the state bird: 1926
Fun fact: The cardinal is named for its color, that of the robes of Roman Catholic cardinals.

State flower common name: Goldenrod
Scientific name: Solidago altissima
Year adopted as the state flower: 1926
Fun fact: There are about one hundred different species of goldenrod, thirty of which are native to Kentucky.

Other state symbols:
State tree: Tulip poplar
State animal: Gray squirrel

"Kentucky"
Cardinal & Goldenrod

LOUISIANA

Received statehood in: 1812
The 18th U.S. state
State population in 1910: 1,656,388
State population in 2010: 4,533,372
State nickname: The Pelican State
State capital: Baton Rouge

State bird common name: Brown pelican
Scientific name: Pelecanus occidentalis
Year adopted as the state bird: 1966
Fun fact: The brown pelican is the only species of
pelican that hunts its prey by watching from the sky
and then plummeting from a great height into the
ocean to catch it.

State flower common name: Magnolia
Scientific name: Magnolia grandiflora
Year adopted as the state flower: 1900
Fun fact: A group of iris admirers tried to have the
magnolia replaced in 1941, to no avail. The iris was
later designated as the state's official wildflower,
however.

Other state symbols:
State tree: Bald cypress
State mammal: Louisiana black bear

"Louisiana"
Brown Pelican & Magnolia

MAINE

Received statehood in: 1820
The 23rd U.S. state
State population in 1910: 742,371
State population in 2010: 1,328,361
State nickname: The Pine Tree State
State capital: Augusta

State bird common name: Black-capped chickadee
Scientific name: Poecile atricapillus
Year adopted as the state bird: 1927
Fun fact: This species mates for life.

State flower common name: White pine cone and tassel
Scientific name: Pinus strobus L.
Year adopted as the state flower: 1895
Fun fact: The pine cone and tassel are not classified
botanically as a flower.

Other state symbols:
State tree: Eastern white pine
State mammal: Moose

"Maine"
Black-capped Chickadee & White Pine Cone Tassel

MARYLAND

Received statehood in: 1788
The 7th U.S. state
State population in 1910: 1,295,346
State population in 2010: 5,773,552
State nickname: The Old Line State
State capital: Annapolis

State bird common name: Baltimore oriole
Scientific name: Icterus galbula
Year adopted as the state bird: 1947
Fun fact: Maryland's major league baseball team is named after this bird.

State flower common name: Black-eyed Susan
Scientific name: Rudbeckia hirta
Year adopted as the state flower: 1918
Fun fact: The Black-eyed Susan is a member of the sunflower family.

Other state symbols:
State tree: White oak tree
State reptile: Diamondback terrapin

"Maryland"
Baltimore Oriole & Black-Eyed Susan

MASSACHUSETTS

Received statehood in: 1788
The 6th U.S. state
State population in 1910: 3,366,416
State population in 2010: 6,547,629
State nickname: The Bay State
State capital: Boston

State bird common name: Black-capped chickadee
Scientific name: Poecile atricapillus
Year adopted as the state bird: 1941
Fun fact: This species is nonmigratory.

State flower common name: Mayflower
Scientific name: Epigaea repens
Year adopted as the state flower: 1918
Also known as: Ground laurel
Fun fact: The children of Massachusetts voted to select
the state flower, and the mayflower won out over the
water lily.

Other state symbols:
State tree: American elm
State mammal: Right whale

"Massachusetts"
Black-capped Chickadee & Mayflower

MICHIGAN

Received statehood in: 1837
The 26th U.S. state
State population in 1910: 2,810,173
State population in 2010: 9,883,640
State nickname: The Great Lakes State
State capital: Lansing

State bird common name: American Robin
Scientific name: Turdus migratorius
Year adopted as the state bird: 1931
Fun fact: A group of students once campaigned to
replace the robin with the Kirtland's warbler, a bird that
is found only in Michigan.

State flower common name: Apple blossom
Scientific name: Pyrus coronaria
Year adopted as the state flower: 1897
Fun fact: Michigan is the second-largest apple producer
in the country.

Other state symbols:
State tree: Eastern white pine
State mammal: White-tailed deer

"Michigan"
American Robin & Apple Blossom

MINNESOTA

Received statehood in: 1858
The 32nd U.S. state
State population in 1910: 2,075,708
State population in 2010: 5,303,925
State nickname: The North Star State
State capital: Saint Paul

State bird common name: Common loon
Scientific name: Gavia immer
Year adopted as the state bird: 1961
Also known as: Great northern diver
Fun fact: Loons that summer on the lakes of Minnesota
migrate south and east to spend the winter along the
Atlantic Coast and the Gulf of Mexico.

State flower common name: Pink Lady's slipper
Scientific name: Cypripedium reginae
Year adopted as the state flower: 1902
Fun fact: The lady slipper is protected by state law.
It is illegal to pick or uproot it.

Other state symbols:
State tree: Red pine
State reptile: Blanding's turtle

"Minnesota"
Common Loon & Pink Lady's Slipper

MISSISSIPPI

Received statehood in: 1817
The 20th U.S. state
State population in 1910: 1,797,114
State population in 2010: 2,967,297
State nickname: The Magnolia State
State capital: Jackson

State bird common name: Mockingbird
Scientific name: Mimus polyglottos
Year adopted as the state bird: 1944
Fun fact: A very common bird in the southeastern
United States, it is also the state bird of Texas,
Arkansas, Tennessee, and Florida.

State flower common name: Magnolia
Scientific name: Magnolia grandiflora
Year adopted as the state flower: 1952
Fun fact: The large blooms can be nearly a foot wide.

Other state symbols:
State insect: Honeybee
State mammal: White-tailed deer

"Mississippi"
Mockingbird & Magnolia

MISSOURI

Received statehood in: 1821
The 24th U.S. state
State population in 1910: 3,293,335
State population in 2010: 5,988,927
State nickname: The Show Me State
State capital: Jefferson City

State bird common name: Eastern bluebird
Scientific name: Sialia sialis
Year adopted as the state bird: 1927
Fun fact: The habitat range of the eastern bluebird
stretches from southern Canada to Central America.

State flower common name: Hawthorn
Scientific name: Crataegus
Year adopted as the state flower: 1923
Fun fact: The hawthorn blossom grows on a deciduous
tree called the white haw.

Other state symbols:
State tree: Flowering dogwood
State animal: Missouri mule

"Missouri"
Eastern Bluebird & Hawthorn

MONTANA

Received statehood in: 1889
The 41st U.S. state
State population in 1910: 376,053
State population in 2010: 989,415
State nickname: Big Sky Country
State capital: Helena

State bird common name: Western meadowlark
Scientific name: Sturnella neglecta
Year adopted as the state bird: 1931
Fun fact: The nests of these birds are intricately woven into vegetation close to the ground.

State flower common name: Bitterroot
Scientific name: Lewisia rediviva
Year adopted as the state flower: 1895
Fun fact: The root of this flower was once used as food by Native Americans.

Other state symbols:
State tree: Ponderosa pine
State mammal: Grizzly bear

"Montana"
Western Meadowlark & Bitterroot

NEBRASKA

Received statehood in: 1867
The 37th U.S. state
State population in 1910: 1,192,214
State population in 2010: 1,826,341
State nickname: The Cornhusker State
State capital: Lincoln

State bird common name: Western meadowlark
Scientific name: Sturnella neglecta
Year adopted as the state bird: 1929
Fun fact: Common to the western United States, the western meadowlark is also the state bird of Wyoming, Kansas, Montana, Oregon, and North Dakota.

State flower common name: Goldenrod
Scientific name: Solidago gigantea
Year adopted as the state flower: 1895
Fun fact: The goldenrod blooms in late summer through early autumn.

Other state symbols:
State tree: Cottonwood
State mammal: White-tailed deer

"Nebraska"
Western Meadowlark & Goldenrod

NEVADA

Received statehood in: 1864
The 36th U.S. state
State population in 1910: 81,875
State population in 2010: 2,700,551
State nickname: The Silver State
State capital: Carson City

State bird common name: Mountain bluebird
Scientific name: Sialia currucoides
Year adopted as the state bird: 1967
Fun fact: The mountain bluebird is a member of the thrush family.

State flower common name: Sagebrush
Scientific name: Artemisia tridentata
Year adopted as the state flower: 1917
Fun fact: The sagebrush produces bright yellow blossoms at the tips of its branches in late summer and early fall.

Other state symbols:
State tree: Single-leaf piñon
State mammal: Desert bighorn sheep

"Nevada"
Mountain Bluebird & Sagebrush

NEW HAMPSHIRE

Received statehood in: 1788
The 9th U.S. state
State population in 1910: 430,572
State population in 2010: 1,316,470
State nickname: The Granite State
State capital: Concord

State bird common name: Purple finch
Scientific name: Carpodacus purpureus
Year adopted as the state bird: 1957
Fun fact: The purple finch won the vote for state bird
over the New Hampshire hen.

State flower common name: Lilac
Scientific name: Syringa vulgaris
Year adopted as the state flower: 1919
Fun fact: The lilac is a member of the olive family.

Other state symbols:
State tree: White birch
State mammal: White-tailed deer

"New Hampshire"
Purple Finch & Lilac

NEW JERSEY

Received statehood in: 1787
The 3rd U.S. state
State population in 1910: 2,537,167
State population in 2010: 8,791,894
State nickname: The Garden State
State capital: Trenton

State bird common name: American goldfinch
Scientific name: Carduelis tristis
Year adopted as the state bird: 1935
Also known as: Eastern goldfinch, wild canary
Fun fact: The American goldfinch's diet is made up almost entirely of seeds.

State flower common name: Violet
Scientific name: Viola sororia
Year adopted as the state flower: 1913
Also known as: Common meadow violet
Fun fact: Although it was originally selected as the state flower in 1913, the violet did not gain official recognition until 1971.

Other state symbols:
State tree: Red oak
State animal: Horse

"New Jersey"
American Goldfinch & Violet

NEW MEXICO

Received statehood in: 1912
The 47th U.S. state
State population in 1910: 327,301
State population in 2010: 2,059,179
State nickname: The Land of Enchantment
State capital: Santa Fe

State bird common name: Greater roadrunner
Scientific name: Geococcyx californianus
Year adopted as the state bird: 1949
Fun fact: A member of the cuckoo family, the roadrunner prefers running to flying.

State flower common name: Yucca
Scientific name: Yucca
Year adopted as the state flower: 1927
Fun fact: The yucca is a member of the lily family.

Other state symbols:
State tree: Pinyon pine
State animal: Black bear

"New Mexico"
Greater Roadrunner & Yucca

NEW YORK

Received statehood in: 1788
The 11th U.S. state
State population in 1910: 9,113,614
State population in 2010: 19,378,102
State nickname: The Empire State
State capital: Albany

State bird common name: Eastern bluebird
Scientific name: Sialia sialis
Year adopted as the state bird: 1970
Fun fact: The eastern bluebird won out over the robin
for the designation of state bird.

State flower common name: Rose
Scientific name: Rosa
Year adopted as the state flower: 1955
Fun fact: Although the rose was chosen as the state
flower in 1891, it wasn't officially designated until 1955.

Other state symbols:
State tree: Sugar maple
State animal: Beaver

"New York"
Eastern Bluebird & Rose

NORTH CAROLINA

Received statehood in: 1789
The 12th U.S. state
State population in 1910: 2,206,287
State population in 2010: 9,535,483
State nickname: The Tar Heel State
State capital: Raleigh

State bird common name: Cardinal
Scientific name: Richmondena cardinalis cardinalis
Year adopted as the state bird: 1943
Fun fact: The cardinal is the most popular state bird,
representing seven states.

State flower common name: Flowering dogwood
Scientific name: Cornus florida
Year adopted as the state flower: 1941
Fun fact: The dogwood blooms from early spring to
midsummer.

Other state symbols:
State tree: Pine
State mammal: Gray squirrel

"North Carolina"
Cardinal & Flowering Dogwood

NORTH DAKOTA

Received statehood in: 1889
The 39th U.S. state
State population in 1910: 577,056
State population in 2010: 672,591
State nickname: The Peace Garden State
State capital: Bismarck

State bird common name: Western meadowlark
Scientific name: Sturnella neglecta
Year adopted as the state bird: 1947
Fun fact: The western meadowlark has a varied diet that consists of plants and insects.

State flower common name: Wild prairie rose
Scientific name: Rosa blanda
Year adopted as the state flower: 1907
Fun fact: The wild rose is native to North America.

Other state symbols:
State tree: American elm
State Horse: Nokota horse

"North Dakota"
Western Meadowlark & Wild Prairie Rose

OHIO

Received statehood in: 1803
The 17th U.S. state
State population in 1910: 4,767,121
State population in 2010: 11,536,504
State nickname: The Buckeye State
State capital: Columbus

State bird common name: Cardinal
Scientific name: Richmondena cardinalis cardinalis
Year adopted as the state bird: 1933
Fun fact: The cardinal breeds more than once in a
season, and the male cares for the first set of hatchlings
while the female lays the second set of eggs.

State flower common name: Scarlet carnation
Scientific name: Dianthus caryophyllus
Year adopted as the state flower: 1904
Fun fact: The scarlet carnation was selected in honor
of President McKinley, who had been a congressional
representative of Ohio and who favored the flower.

Other state symbols:
State tree: Ohio buckeye
State mammal: White-tailed deer

"Ohio"
Cardinal & Scarlet Carnation

OKLAHOMA

Received statehood in: 1907
The 46th U.S. state
State population in 1910: 1,657,155
State population in 2010: 3,751,351
State nickname: The Sooner State
State capital: Oklahoma City

State bird common name: Scissor-tailed flycatcher
Scientific name: *Tyrannus forficatus*
Year adopted as state bird: 1951
Also known as: Swallow-tailed flycatcher
Fun fact: The bird is named for its affinity for
consuming flying insects.

State flower common name: Oklahoma rose
Scientific name: Phoradendron flavescens
Year adopted as the state flower: 2004
Fun fact: The Oklahoma rose was named the official
state flower in 2004. Before that year, mistletoe had
been the state flower.

Other state symbols:
State tree: Redbud
State mammal: Mexican free-tailed bat

"Oklahoma"
Scissor-tailed Flycatcher & Oklahoma Rose

OREGON

Received statehood in: 1859
The 33rd U.S. state
State population in 1910: 672,765
State population in 2010: 3,831,074
State nickname: The Beaver State
State capital: Salem

State bird common name: Western meadowlark
Scientific name: Sturnella neglecta
Year adopted as the state bird: 1927
Fun fact: The female bird usually builds the nest
without the help of the male.

State flower common name: Oregon grape
Scientific name: Mahonia aquifolium
Year adopted as the state flower: 1899
Fun fact: The name comes from the yellow blooms that
develop into berries resembling a cluster of grapes.

Other state symbols:
State tree: Douglas fir
State mammal: Beaver

"Oregon"
Western Meadowlark & Oregon Grape

PENNSYLVANIA

Received statehood in: 1787
The 2nd U.S. state
State population in 1910: 7,665,111
State population in 2010: 12,702,379
State nickname: The Keystone State
State capital: Harrisburg

State bird common name: Ruffed grouse
Scientific name: Bonasa umbellus
Year adopted as the state bird: 1931
Fun fact: The ruffed grouse is technically considered
the state game bird of Pennsylvania. There is no official
state bird.

State flower common name: Mountain laurel
Scientific name: Kalmia latifolia
Year adopted as the state flower: 1933
Fun fact: A member of the heath family of shrubs, the
mountain laurel is a relative of the rhododendron.

Other state symbols:
State tree: Eastern hemlock
State mammal: White-tailed deer

"Pennsylvania"
Ruffed Grouse & Mountain Laurel

RHODE ISLAND

Received statehood in: 1790
The 13th U.S. state
State population in 1910: 542,610
State population in 2010: 1,052,567
State nickname: The Ocean State
State capital: Providence

State bird common name: Rhode Island red
Scientific name: Gallus gallus domesticus
Year adopted as the state bird: 1954
Fun fact: The Rhode Island red, a domesticated chicken, got its name because it was originally bred in the state.

State flower common name: Violet
Scientific name: Viola
Year adopted as the state flower: 1968
Fun fact: The violet was selected to represent Rhode Island in 1897 but was not officially adopted until 1968.

Other state symbols:
State tree: Red maple
State fish: Striped bass

"Rhode Island"
Rhode Island Red & Violet

SOUTH CAROLINA

Received statehood in: 1788
The 8th U.S. state
State population in 1910: 1,515,400
State population in 2010: 4,625,364
State nickname: The Palmetto State
State capital: Columbia

State bird common name: Carolina wren
Scientific name: Thryothorus ludovicianus
Year adopted as the state bird: 1948
Fun fact: The mockingbird was declared the state bird in
1939, but that decision was overturned in 1948 and the
Carolina wren took its place.

State flower common name: Yellow jessamine
Scientific name: Gelsemium sempervirens
Year adopted as the state flower: 1924
Also known as: Evening trumpet-flower
Fun fact: Native to South Carolina, the yellow jessamine
is a fragrant flower whose essential oils are often used
for hair and perfume products.

Other state symbols:
State tree: Sabal palmetto
State mammal: White-tailed deer

"South Carolina"
Carolina Wren & Yellow Jessamine

SOUTH DAKOTA

Received statehood in: 1889
The 40th U.S. state
State population in 1910: 583,888
State population in 2010: 814,180
State nickname: Mount Rushmore State
State capital: Pierre

State bird common name: Ring-necked pheasant
Scientific name: Phasianus colchicus
Year adopted as the state bird: 1943
Fun fact: Originally from China, the ring-necked pheasant is one of the world's most hunted birds.

State flower common name: Pasque flower
Scientific name: Pulsatilla hirsutissima
Year adopted as the state flower: 1903
Also known as: Prairie crocus, meadow anemone, wind flower
Fun fact: The flower was chosen because it is a herald of spring for the state.

Other state symbols:
State tree: Black Hills spruce
State animal: Coyote

"South Dakota"
Ring-Necked Pheasant & Pasque Flower

TENNESSEE

Received statehood in: 1796
The 16th U.S. state
State population in 1910: 2,184,789
State population in 2010: 6,346,105
State nickname: The Volunteer State
State capital: Nashville

State bird common name: Mockingbird
Scientific name: Mimus polyglottos
Year adopted as the state bird: 1933
Fun fact: During a vote to select the state bird, the mockingbird won out over the robin by a slim margin.

State flower common name: Iris
Scientific name: Iris pseudacorus
Year adopted as the state flower: 1933
Fun fact: The iris shares the title of state flower with the passionflower. The iris is the state's cultivated flower and the passionflower is the state's wildflower.

Other state symbols:
State tree: Tulip poplar
State mammal: Raccoon

"Tennessee"
Mockingbird & Iris

TEXAS

Received statehood in: 1845
The 28th U.S. state
State population in 1910: 3,896,542
State population in 2010: 25,145,561
State nickname: The Lone Star State
State capital: Austin

State bird common name: Mockingbird
Scientific name: Mimus polyglottos
Year adopted as the state bird: 1927
Fun fact: One reason the mockingbird was selected is that it can be found all over the state.

State flower common name: Bluebonnet
Scientific name: Lupinus subcarnosus
Year adopted as the state flower: 1901
Also known as: Buffalo clover
Fun fact: Other proposed options for the state flower symbol were the open cotton boll and the prickly pear cactus.

Other state symbols:
State tree: Pecan
State mammal: Texas longhorn

"Texas"
Mockingbird & Bluebonnet

UTAH

Received statehood in: 1896
The 45th U.S. state
State population in 1910: 373,351
State population in 2010: 2,763,885
State nickname: The Beehive State
State capital: Salt Lake City

State bird common name: California gull
Scientific name: Larus californicus
Year adopted as the state bird: 1955
Fun fact: The gull was chosen as the state bird for its historical role in preventing the destruction of crops by insects in what is now Salt Lake City.

State flower common name: Sego lily
Scientific name: Calochortus nuttallii
Year adopted as the state flower: 1911
Also known as: Mariposa lily
Fun fact: The root of the plant was at one time used as food by the people of Utah during a food shortage.

Other state symbols:
State tree: Blue spruce
State mammal: Rocky Mountain elk

"Utah"
California Gull & Sego Lily

VERMONT

Received statehood in: 1791
The 14th U.S. state
State population in 1910: 355,956
State population in 2010: 625,741
State nickname: The Green Mountain State
State capital: Montpelier

State bird common name: Hermit thrush
Scientific name: Hylocichla guttata
Year adopted as the state bird: 1941
Fun fact: The hermit thrush was chosen to symbolize
Vermont despite protests from some who felt that the
blue jay or crow were more representative of the state.

State flower common name: Red clover
Scientific name: Trifolium pratense
Year adopted as the state flower: 1894
Fun fact: The red clover is a member of the legume
family.

Other state symbols:
State tree: Sugar maple
State mammal: Morgan horse

"Vermont"
Hermit Thrush & Red Clover

VIRGINIA

Received statehood in: 1788
The 10th U.S. state
State population in 1910: 2,061,612
State population in 2010: 8,001,024
State nickname: The Old Dominion State
State capital: Richmond

State bird common name: Cardinal
Scientific name: Richmondena cardinalis cardinalis
Year adopted as the state bird: 1950
Fun fact: The study of cardinal songs has revealed the development of accents that vary from one region to another.

State flower common name: Flowering dogwood
Scientific name: Cornus florida
Year adopted as the state flower: 1918
Also know as: American dogwood
Fun fact: Virginia is the only state to have designated the same flower and tree as its symbols.

Other state symbols:
State tree: Dogwood
State fish: Brook trout

"Virginia"
Cardinal & Flowering Dogwood

WASHINGTON

Received statehood in: 1889
The 42nd U.S. state
State population in 1910: 1,141,990
State population in 2010: 6,724,540
State nickname: The Evergreen State
State capital: Olympia

State bird common name: American goldfinch
Scientific name: Carduelis tristis
Year adopted as the state bird: 1951
Also known as: Eastern goldfinch, wild canary, willow goldfinch
Fun fact: The state bird originally selected by the schoolchildren of Washington was the western meadowlark. But because so many other states had chosen the same bird, the state legislature rejected their choice and designated the American goldfinch in its place.

State flower common name: Coast rhododendron
Scientific name: Rhododendron macrophyllum
Year adopted as the state flower: 1959
Fun fact: Although the rhododendron had been voted on and approved as the state flower in 1893, it was not made official until 1959.

Other state symbols:
State tree: Western hemlock
State mammal: Orca whale

"Washington"
American Goldfinch & Coast Rhododendron

WEST VIRGINIA

Received statehood in: 1863
The 35th U.S. state
State population in 1910: 1,221,119
State population in 2010: 1,852,994
State nickname: The Mountain State
State capital: Charleston

State bird common name: Cardinal
Scientific name: Richmondena cardinalis cardinalis
Year adopted as state bird: 1949
Fun fact: Another option for state bird at one time was
the tufted titmouse.

State flower common name: Rhododendron
Scientific name: Rhododendron maximum
Year adopted as the state flower: 1903
Also known as: Big laurel
Fun fact: The rhododendron was designated the state
flower of West Virginia after it won over the goldenrod
by a landslide in a statewide referendum.

Other state symbols:
State tree: Sugar maple
State animal: Black bear

"West Virginia"
Cardinal & Rhododendron

WISCONSIN

Received statehood in: 1848
The 30th U.S. state
State population in 1910: 2,333,860
State population in 2010: 5,686,986
State nickname: The Badger State
State capital: Madison

State bird common name: American Robin
Scientific name: Turdus migratorius
Year adopted as the state bird: 1949
Fun fact: The robin can breed successfully up to three
times a year.

State flower common name: Wood violet
Scientific name: Viola papilionacea
Year adopted as the state flower: 1909
Fun fact: During a statewide contest on Arbor Day in
1909, the violet won out over the wild rose as the state
flower.

Other state symbols:
State tree: Sugar maple
State mammal: Badger

"Wisconsin"
American Robin & Wood Violet

WYOMING

Received statehood in: 1890
The 44th U.S. state
State population in 1910: 145,965
State population in 2010: 563,626
State nickname: The Cowboy State
State capital: Cheyenne

State bird common name: Western meadowlark
Scientific name: Sturnella neglecta
Year adopted as the state bird: 1927
Fun fact: The western meadowlark is a member of the blackbird family, but it has a unique, bright yellow belly and a black triangular collar.

State flower common name: Indian paintbrush
Scientific name: Castilleja linariaefolia
Year adopted as the state flower: 1917
Also known as: Prairie fire
Fun fact: The Indian paintbrush is a parasitic plant.

Other state symbols:
State tree: Plains cottonwood
State mammal: Buffalo

"Wyoming"
Western Meadowlark & Indian Paintbrush

SOURCES

www.50states.com
www.demographia.com/db-state1900.htm
www.census.gov
www.statesymbolsusa.org
www.americanmeadows.com
www. netstate.com
www.allaboutbirds.org
www.proflowers.com